POETRY *in motion 2*

ALAN BENNETT
GERMAINE GREER
JOHN MORTIMER
A.S. BYATT

Published in 1992 by Channel 4 Television
60 Charlotte Street London W1P 2AX

Produced by Broadcasting Support Services to accompany POETRY IN MOTION (2nd series) (a Lilyville Production for Channel 4, produced by Tony Cash), first shown on Channel 4 in November–December 1992

Editor: Derek Jones
Editorial consultant: Nancy Duin
Designer: BIG-i, London.
Printer: The Good News Press
Distributed by Broadcasting Support Services

Broadcasting Support Services is an educational charity, which runs helplines and provides follow-up services for viewers and listeners.

For further copies, please send a cheque or postal order for £3.25 (made payable to Channel 4 Television) to:

POETRY IN MOTION II
PO Box 4000
London W3 6XJ or Cardiff CF5 2XT

Acknowledgements

Channel 4 Television and Broadcasting Support Services would like to thank the following individuals and publishers for their permission to reproduce some of the poetry in this book: the Estate of Frances Cornford for `Childhood' from *Collected Poems*, published by the Cresset Press; Gavin Ewart for `Brilliant Spy and Totally Inadequate Man' from *Collected Poems 1933–1980*, published by Hutchinson Ltd; Faber & Faber Ltd for Seamus Heaney's `Man and Boy', and for W. H. Auden's `Letter to Lord Byron' and `In Memory of Sigmund Freud', both reprinted from *The Collected Poems of W. H. Auden*, edited by Edward Mendelson; Andrei Voznesensky for `War' (trans. William Jay Smith & Vera Dunham); John Murray (Publishers) Ltd for the extract from John Betjeman's *Summoned by Bells* and for the extract from Alfred Noyes' *The Highwayman* from his *Collected Poems;* Oxford University Press for Peter Porter's `An Exequy' from his *Collected Poems* (1983); the Estate of William Plomer for `French Lisette: A Ballad of Maida Vale' from *Collected Poems*, published by Jonathan Cape Ltd; Robson Books Ltd for Vernon Scannell's `View from a High Chair'; and the Regents of the University of California for Mary Barnard's translation of 'Ode to Anactoria' from *Sappho: A New Translation* (© 1958 the Regents of the University of California, renewed 1984 Mary Barnard)

PHOTOGRAPHY: Barnabys Picture Library: pages 17, 18. B.F.I: pages 9, 14, 36, 48, 51. Padraig Boyle: pages 60, 61. The Bridgeman Art Library: pages 25, 27, 34, 42, 53, 67. The Hulton Deutsch Collection Ltd: pages 19, 21, 40, 65. Network Photographers: page 12. Caroline Penn: pages 7, 23, 39, 55. Chris Priestley: page 57. Rex Features: page 30.
ILLUSTRATION: page 50: Keith Slote.

CONTENTS

INTRODUCTION

Programme-makers working in the arts have it lucky: they get to meet and collaborate with some of the most talented people around. For me personally, it has been a special pleasure to produce and direct writers as distinguished and committed as the four who have penned our Channel 4 series, *Poetry in Motion*.

I was not surprised that making the programme with them turned out to be such an enjoyable experience. It could hardly have been otherwise when all four share something of Germaine Greer's talent for the divertingly raunchy polemic, John Mortimer's on-the-side-of-the-angels wit and urbanity, A. S. Byatt's knowledge of and passionate dedication to the best in our literary traditions, and Alan Bennett's extraordinary ear for the incongruous and telling vernacular phrase. What I did not anticipate was how instructive and thought-provoking the exercise would prove.

To be involved in the selection of poetry for the general public is to participate in the current debate concerning what of our cultural heritage needs to be preserved and transmitted. Value judgements are quite unavoidable for educationists, arts administrators and public-service broadcasters. Not everything can be given a performance, kept or studied, but it would be perverse not to offer the best of a particular artform, even if `the best' is simply defined as what has given pleasure or exerted influence over time.

For those reasons, I was pleased that, between them, our contributors chose poems written over a span of more than half a millennium. Hitherto, television has accepted a responsibility to the drama and novels of the past – classic plays and adaptations of great works of literature are among the programmes of which British producers can be most proud. However, poetry – both yesterday's and today's – rarely gets a look in.

If, in *Poetry in Motion*, poems from the 19th and 20th centuries are more numerous than earlier ones, I suspect the reason is simply because reading a poem on the page is not the same experience as hearing it recited on air. The language of the 16th and 17th centuries is different enough to cause quite serious problems for the one-time listener. Nevertheless, as A. S. Byatt points out in her programme `In Memoriam', poets often reflect the work of their predecessors. Peter Porter's `An Exequy' is all the more moving for the listener/reader who is acquainted with Bishop Henry King's lament for his dead wife, written more than 300 years earlier.

However, Porter's poem and King's *An Exequy to His Matchless Never to Be Forgotten Friend* are worth knowing for their own sakes, and I was grateful to have them drawn to my attention. Equally, I was delighted to meet William Plomer's `French Lisette', Charles Causley's `Enemy' and Gavin Ewart's `Brilliant Spy . . .', especially as they rub shoulders with Milton's and Shelley's Satan, Alfred Noyes's highwayman and Oscar Wilde's murderer in Reading Gaol. It's not just the range of experience that appeals, but also the variety of tone and literary style.

If, as we hope, viewers and readers find the content of *Poetry in Motion* both enjoyable and stimulating, they might like to weigh up how much of the pleasure is due to the catholic tastes of our contributors and to the fact that the poems represent so many different historical periods. All of us surely need reminders of our common past.

TONY CASH
Producer, *Poetry in Motion*

CHILDHOOD
Alan Bennett

Alan Bennett grew up in Leeds and was educated at Oxford University. Following world-wide success in the satirical review *Beyond the Fringe* (1960), he began to write for the theatre: *Forty Years On* (1968), *Getting On* (1971), *Habeas Corpus* (1973), *The Old Country* (1977). Following his 1965 play *My Father Knew Lloyd George* for the BBC, he has created an impressive body of television work, including: *Sunset Across the Bay* (1975), *The Old Crowd* (1979), *All Day on the Sands* (1979), the *Objects of Affection* series (1982), *An Englishman Abroad* (1983). He also wrote the screenplays for the films *A Private Function* (1984) and *Prick Up Your Ears* (1987). Recent work includes the *Talking Heads* series and *A Question of Attribution* for television, and *The Wind in the Willows* and *The Madness of George III* for the theatre. In 1990, he wrote and presented the first series of *Poetry in Motion*.

'Don't go away,' said little Tom. 'This is so nice. I never had any one to cuddle before.'

'Don't go away,' said all the children. 'You have not sung us one song.'

'Well, I have time for only one,' said the old lady, 'so what shall it be?'

'The doll you lost! The doll you lost!' cried all the babies at once.

So the old lady sang:

I once had a sweet little doll, dears,
The prettiest doll in the world:
Her cheeks were so red and so white, dears,
And her hair was so charmingly curled.
But I lost my poor little doll, dears,
As I played in the heath one day;
And I cried for her more than a week, dears;
But I never could find where she lay.

I found my poor little doll, dears,
As I played in the heath one day:
Folks says she is terribly changed, dears,
For her paint is all washed away,
And her arm trodden off by the cows, dears,
And her hair not the least bit curled;
Yet for old sakes' sake she is still, dears,
The prettiest doll in the world.

From Charles Kingsley's *The Water Babies* (1863)

That is a poem I remember my mother reciting to my brother and me when we were very little. Though it comes from Charles Kingsley's *The Water Babies*, it is not a good poem – shallow, sentimental and silly. But it never failed to reduce me to tears, so that, when my mother was shaping up to say it, I, unlike the water babies, would beg her not to start.

I suppose she liked saying it because it was the only complete poem she knew by heart. The other poetry she remembered tended to be a bit patchy – a verse of this, a line of that – and it always came equipped with the gestures she had acquired when she first learned to recite the pieces in a Halifax schoolroom in the years before the First World War. Poems such as Wordsworth's 'Daffodils by Ullswater' (1807):

I wandered lonely as a cloud
That floats on high o'er vales and hills,
When all at once I saw a crowd,
A host, of golden daffodils . . .

John Greenleaf Whittier's 'Barbara Frietchie':

'Shoot, if you must this old grey head,
But spare your country's flag,' she said . . .

'Who touches a hair of yon grey head
Dies like a dog! March on!' he said . . .

Sir Henry Newbolt's 'Vitae Lampada':

There's a breathless hush in the Close tonight . . .

And

They buried him darkly at dead of night . . .

from 'The Burial of Sir John Moore at Corunna' by Charles Wolfe (1791–1823) – fragments of verse and fragments of fragments, remembered by one generation and fractured again when recalled by the next. Scraps like these are one of the things we mean by the 'poetry of childhood'; education, what's left when we've forgotten everything we ever learned.

P. G. Wodehouse made these vagaries of memory part of his style:

Lord Emsworth was reminded of a Kipling poem the curate had recited at a village entertainment his sister Constance had once made him attend – something about if you can something something and have something something, you'll be a man, my son, or words to that effect.

Galahad at Blandings (1964)

I am possibly not the best person to talk about childhood, though I had one, of course. Looking back, I feel I was much more middle-aged then than I am now. I read biographies and autobiographies backwards – childhood being the last thing I want to know about somebody – and while I have some nostalgia for the world as it was when I was a child, I have none for the frightful little creep I was in it.

Poems by children are hard to come by. One of the attributes of a poet is, after all, the capacity to become a child again, to see things as if for the first time, the world made fresh. So poems about one's early years are almost inevitably poems of recollection or reconstruction. They are not reports from the frontier.

'Childhood,' John Betjeman wrote, 'is measured out in sounds and smells/and sights before the dark of reason grows.' This is a poem that tries to catch that time.

• Kes

VIEW FROM A HIGH CHAIR Vernon Scannell (1922–)

Here thump on tray
With mug and splash
Wet white down there
The sofa purrs
The window squeaks
Bump more with mug
And make voice big
And she will come
Sky in the room
Quiet as a cloud
Flowers in the sky
Come down show soft
But warm as milk
Hide all the things
That squint with shine
That gruff and bite
And want to hurt
Come swallow us
And taste so sweet
As down we go
To try our feet.

Now a poem that spans three generations, in which a son writes about his father and about his father when he was a son.

MAN AND BOY Seamus Heaney (1939–)

Catch the old one first,
(My father's joke was also old, and heavy
And predictable.) Then the young ones
Will all follow, and Bob's your uncle.

On slow bright river evenings, the sweet time
Made him afraid we'd take too much for granted
And so our spirits must be lightly checked.

Blessed be down-to-earth! Blessed be highs!
Blessed be the detachment of dumb love
In that broad-backed, low-set man
Who feared debt all his life, but now and then
Could make a splash like the salmon he said was
'As big as a wee pork pig by the sound of it'.

In earshot of the pool where the salmon jumped
Back through its own unheard concentric
soundwaves
A mower leans forever on his scythe.

He has mown himself to the centre of the field
And stands in a final perfect ring
Of sunlit stubble.

'Go and tell your father,' the mower says
(He said it to my father who told me)
'I have it mowed as clean as a new sixpence.'

My father is a barefoot boy with news,
Running at eye-level with weeds and stooks
On the afternoon of his own father's death.

The open, black half of the half door waits.
I feel much heat and hurry in the air.
I feel his legs and quick heels far away

And strange as my own – when he will piggyback
me
At a great height, light-headed and thin-boned,
Like a witless elder rescued from the fire.

That was the childhood of a poor boy in Ireland. This is childhood in an upper-middle-class household in Cambridge.

CHILDHOOD Frances Cornford (1886–1960)

I used to think that grown up people chose
To have stiff backs and wrinkles round their
nose,
And veins like small fat snakes on either hand,
On purpose to be grand.
Till through the banisters I watched one day
My great aunt Etty's friend who was going away,
And how her onyx beads had come unstrung.

I saw her grope to find them as they rolled;
And then I knew she was helplessly old,
As I was helplessly young.

The 'great aunt Etty' mentioned in that poem was the daughter of Charles Darwin and one of the many Darwin relatives described in Gwen Raverat's book *Period Piece: A Cambridge Childhood* (1952).

> *Aunt Etty* [she wrote] *had learned after her fashion to appreciate poetry . . . but always applied the full measure of her drastic common sense to all the more imaginative passages of the poets . . . Wordsworth was her religion but one was never able to read more than two or three consecutive lines without stopping to discuss exactly what the words meant . . . One of her most engaging habits was to alter a phrase in a poem to suit herself should she not happen to approve of the poet's own version; and if she was not satisfied with her alteration, she would apply to Frances, Margaret or even me to improve it for her.*
>
> *I remember that Wordsworth's 'The wind comes to me from fields of sleep' did not please her. 'What does it mean?' she said. 'Sleep does not grow in fields.'*
>
> *I said, 'Why not try "fields of sheep"?' This was not well received.*

It is a truism of the 20th century that childhood explains all, as in the verse by George William Russell (1867–1935):

In ancient shadows and twilights
Where childhood had strayed,
The world's great sorrows were born
And its heroes were made.
In the lost boyhood of Judas
Christ was betrayed.

From 'Germinal', *Vale and Others Poems* (1931)

There are some children – more and more, one feels, nowadays – who scarcely have childhoods at all. We see them every day on television, trekking to refugee camps, gazing with incomprehension and reproach from the pages of the newspapers.

WAR Andrei Voznesensky (1933–)
(trans. William Jay Smith & Vera Dunham)

With the open eyes of their dead fathers
Toward other worlds they gaze ahead –
Children who, wide-eyed, become
Periscopes of the buried dead.

Sin being of less consequence today, so innocence cuts less ice, too. Certainly poets do not make such a song and dance about the loss of it; innocence is just part of the left luggage of childhood with most people not even bothering to keep the receipt. It is only poets and novelists who go back and try and find what it was they lost all those years ago. All too often it was a myth.

'The minds of children,' wrote E. F. Benson (1867–1940),

have those diseases incident to childhood much as their bodies have. I had had my measles of sentimentality and had got over it, but I developed during this year a kind of whooping cough of lying.

Cruelty in childhood can be like that. Children can be cruel to each other, to pets, to anything or anyone weaker than themselves. With luck (or love), this cruelty is a phase that inoculates them against a lifetime of the same.

This poem is called 'On shooting a swallow in early youth' and is by the Victorian poet Charles Turner.

I hoard a little spring of secret tears
For thee, poor bird; thy death-blow was my crime;
From the far past it has flow'd on for years;
It never dries; it brims at swallow-time.
No kindly voice within me took thy part,
Till I stood o'er thy last faint flutterings;
Since then, methinks, I have a gentler heart,
And gaze with pity on all wounded wings.
Full oft the vision of thy fallen head,
Twittering in highway dust, appeals to me;
Thy helpless form, as when I struck thee dead,
Drops from every swallow-flight I see.
I would not have thine airy spirit laid,
I seem to love the little ghost I made.

It is lucky that it was only a swallow the boy had been cruel to, rather than learning his lesson on one of his fellows, another human being. To be 'learned on' (which is not the same as teaching) can be no fun at all at the time, and not much consolation later, 'you taught me a lot' often just meaning that you were the paper I learned to scribble on, the branch on which I got to sharpen my knife.

One of life's such victims – as he saw it, anyway – was John Betjeman (1906–84). This is part of his long autobiographical poem *Summoned by Bells* (1960):

Percival Mandeville, the perfect boy,
Was all a schoolmaster could wish to see –
Upright and honourable, good at games,
Well-built, blue eyed; a sense of leadership
Lifted him head and shoulders from the crowd:
His work was good. His written answers, made
In a round, tidy and decided hand,
Pleased the examiners. His open smile
Enchanted others. He could also frown
On anything unsporting, mean or base,
Unworthy of the spirit of the school
And what it stood for. Oh the dreadful hour
When once upon a time he frowned on me!
Just what had happened I cannot recall –
Maybe some bullying in the dormitory;
But well I recollect his warning words:

'I'll fight you, Betjeman, you swine, for that,
Behind the bike shed before morning school.'
So all the previous night I spewed with fear.
I could not box: I greatly dreaded pain.
A recollection of the winding punch
Jack Drayton once delivered, blows and boots
Upon the bum at Highgate Junior School,
All multiplied by X from Mandeville,
Emptied my bladder. Silent in the dorm
I cleaned my teeth and clambered into bed.
Thin seemed pyjamas and inadequate
The regulation blankets once so warm.
'What's up?' 'Oh, nothing.' I expect they knew . . .
And, in the morning, cornflakes, bread and tea,
Cook's Farm Eggs and a spoon of marmalade,
Which heralded the North and Hillard hours
Of Latin composition, brought the post.
Breakfast and letters! Then it was a flash
Of hope, escape and inspiration came:
Invent a letter of bad news from home.
I hung my head and tried to look as though,
By keeping such a brave stiff upper lip
And just not blubbing, I was noble too.
I sought out Mandeville. 'I say,' I said,
'I'm frightfully sorry I can't fight today.
I've just received some rotten news from home:
My mater's very ill.' No need for more –
His arm was round my shoulder comforting:
'All right, old chap. Of course I understand.'

W. H. Auden (1907–1973) left an account of his childhood in verse as part of that unusual travel book he wrote with Louis McNeice, *Letters from Iceland* (1937), where it occurs in the form of 'a letter to Lord Byron'.

I must admit that I was most precocious
(Precocious children rarely grow up good).
My aunts and uncles thought me quite atrocious
For using words more adult than I should;
My first remark at school did all it could
To shake a matron's monumental poise;
'I like to see the various types of boys.'

• • •

I hate the modern trick, to tell the truth,
Of straightening out the kinks in the young mind,
Our passion for the tender plant of youth,
Our hatred for all weeds of any kind.

Slogans are bad: the best that I can find
Is this: 'Let each child have that's in our care
As much neurosis as the child can bear.

• • •

We all grow up the same way, more or less;
Life is not known to give away her presents;
She only swops. The unselfconsciousness
That children share with animals and peasants
Sinks in the Sturm und Drang *of adolescence.*
Like other boys I lost my taste for sweets,
Discovered sunsets, passion, God, and Keats.

I shall recall a single incident,
No more. I spoke of mining engineering
As the career on which my mind was bent,
But for some time my fancies had been veering;
Mirages of the future kept appearing;
Crazes had come and gone in short, sharp gales,
For motor-bikes, photography, and whales.

But indecision broke off with a clean cut end
One afternoon in March at half past three
When walking in a ploughed field with a friend;
Kicking a little stone, he turned to me
And said, 'Tell me, do you write poetry?'
I never had, and said so, but I knew
That very moment what I wished to do.

From *A Letter to Lord Byron*

Some critics of Auden have said that it took him a long time to escape his childhood. In this connection, it is worth noting (or perhaps not worth noting at all) that the personnel of his poems and their settings – spies, gangs, garden fêtes, lecturers, lunatics, dogs, vicars, authors, spinsters, pageants, psychologists, bachelors, Bolsheviks, secret societies and cranks generally – are, category for category, the cast and personnel of the *William* books by Richmal Crompton – William, like Auden, another character who never grew up.

If one wanted to be cheeky, one could say that Auden's primacy among his contemporaries was not unlike William's leadership of The Outlaws – Sherwood, Spender and McNeice being the Ginger, Douglas and Henry of poetry in the Thirties. But that, as I say, is neither here nor there.

A poet whose experience comes close to my own, both in location and language, is Tony Harrison (1937–).

Like me, he was brought up in Leeds in the Forties, and this is a poem about doing his homework in the front room. (Incidentally, a 'damascener' is a metal worker.)

STUDY Tony Harrison

Best clock. Best carpet. Best three chairs.
For death, for Christmases, a houseless aunt,
for those too old or sick to manage stairs.

I try to whistle but I can't.

Uncle Joe came here to die. His gaping jaws
once plugged in to the power of his stammer
patterned the stuck plosive without pause
like a d-d-d-damascener's hammer.

My aunty's baby still. The dumbstruck mother
The mirror, tortoise-shell-like celluloid
held to it, passed from one hand to another.
No babble, blubber, breath. The glass won't
cloud.

The best clock's only wound for layings out
so the stillness isn't tapped by its ticks.
The settee's shapeless underneath its shroud.

My mind moves upon silence and Aeneid VI.

What I remember of our front room was the settee, the end of which let down, revealing in just one strip the bright original colours of the velvet when it was first bought. 'Your swotting' was what my homework was called, and even when I started to write plays, that was still 'your swotting', too.

For Tony Harrison and for me, literature – or, at any rate, education – meant liberation. Some children are less fortunate.

MY ENEMY Charles Causley (1917–)

My enemy was the pork butcher's son.
I see him, head and shoulders above me,
Sphinx-faced, his cheeks the colour of lard, the eyes
Revolver-blue through Bunter spectacles.
When we lined up for five to nine school
He'd get behind me, crumple up a fist,
Stone thumb between the first and second fingers;
Punch out a tune across my harp of ribs.

Ten years ahead of Chamberlain, I tried
Appeasement, with the same results; gave him
My lunch of bread and cheese, the Friday bun,
The Lucky Bags we bought at Maggie Snell's.
One Armistice I wept through the Two Minutes
Because my dad was killed in France (not true).
'Poor little sod, his father's dead', my enemy
Observed, discreetly thumping me again.
I took the scholarship exam not for
The promise of Latin, Greek, but to escape
My enemy. The pork butcher's sharp son
Passed too, and I remember how my heart
Fell like a bucket down a summer well
The day Boss Ward read out our names. And how,
Quite unaccountably, the torment stopped
Once we were at the Grammar. We've not met

Since 1939, although I heard
How as a gunner in the long retreat
Hauling the pieces from Burma, he was met
At the first village by naked kids with stones,
Placards reading 'Quit India'. After that,
Nothing; except our pair of sentences
To thirty years in chalk Siberias:
Which one of us is which hard to define
For children in the butcher's class, and mine.

One (to me) disquieting feature of programmes such as *Poetry in Motion* – as distinct from writing plays or, I imagine, novels and certainly poems – is that one is keen to show how clever one is. This is true of literary criticism in general. The element of 'showing off' is very much part of it – understandably, I suppose, because if you cannot be seen to know a lot, your opinion is not worth having in the first place. Still, such displays of wide reading or erudition are pretty discouraging both to reader and viewer, so I would like to say that, before I undertook *Poetry in Motion 2*, I knew only a couple of these poems. They did not come 'out of stock', as it were, and of course, I knew none of them by heart.

Learning by heart was already out of fashion when I was at school, so the only verses I have by heart, learned by dint of repetition and use, are *Hymns Ancient and Modern*. Lately there has been some attempt to return to learning by heart, which, in principle, I would be in favour of, while dubious of the 'Victorian values' brigade from which it comes. I feel that the most fervent proponents of learning by heart have other lessons their hearts could learn first.

The poems that children half remember nowadays are less likely to be the 'Quinquireme of Nineveh from distant Ophir' type of stuff, the 'standards', if you like – though, of course, they are not standards now, more golden oldies. What children are likely to know snatches of are the poems of Roger McGough or Brian Patten, just as their parents may only recall the lyrics of Bob Dylan. I do not mean that one thing is just as good as another if I say that I do not think it much matters what you have by heart as long as you have something – a page of *Wisden*, the dialogue from *Casablanca*, the 'Parrot Sketch' or even a television jingle. They all tell you something about words and go to thicken the cerebral soup.

Childhood is, I suppose, a journey that kicks off with the womb and trails off around puberty, and nowadays it is not quite the long haul it was when I was young. Still, it is a period no writer can escape, and as Flannery O'Connor has said, 'Anybody who has survived childhood has enough information about life to last them the rest of their days.'

At the end of childhood is when I find children are generally at their worst, fit only for each other's company. So it is appropriate that I should end with part of a poem that I do not altogether like but which expresses the self-absorbed exuberance and the way young people have of being thoroughly pleased with themselves for no particular reason, which nowadays I

find so irritating. Of course, I do not remember being in the least like that myself.

We two boys together clinging
One the other never leaving,
Up and down the roads going,
North and South excursions making,
Power enjoying, elbows stretching, fingers
clutching,
Arm'd and fearless, eating, drinking, sleeping,
loving,
No law less than ourselves owning, sailing,
soldiering, thieving, threatening,
Misers, menials, priests alarming, air breathing,
water drinking, on the turf or the sea-beach
dancing
Cities wrenching, east scorning, statutes
mocking, feebleness chasing,
Fulfilling our foray

From Walt Whitman (1819–92), *Leaves of Grass*

FURTHER READING

Dawn and Dusk: Poems of Our Times for Boys and Girls,
introduced by Charles Causley
(Brockhampton Press 1962).

Period Piece: A Cambridge Childhood
by Gwen Raverat (Faber 1952).

The Rattle Bag,
edited by Seamus Heaney & Ted Hughes
(Faber 1982).

Spells for Poets: An Anthology of Words and Comments,
edited by F. McEachran
(Garnstone Press 1974).

The Wild Wave,
compiled by H. S. Houghton-Hawksley & A. B. S. Eaton
(John Murray Ltd 1982).

WOMEN
IN LOVE
Germaine Greer

Germaine Greer was born in Melbourne, Australia and studied at the universities of Melbourne, Sydney and Cambridge. She has taught English literature at Warwick University (1968–73) and the University of Tulsa (1980–83) and is now Special Lecturer and unofficial Fellow at Newnham College, Cambridge. She writes and broadcasts widely. Her first book *The Female Eunuch* (1970) was an international bestseller. She is also the author of *The Obstacle Race, Sex and Destiny, The Madwoman's Underclothes, Daddy, we hardly knew you* and *The Change*, and is the co-editor of *Kissing the Rod*. She has lived in the United Kingdom since 1964, and now resides in Essex.

In all literate societies, the idea of poetry has been inextricable from the idea of love. It is almost as if that particular type of patterned utterance is itself a mating call of some kind. The poet celebrates the beauty of the beloved and he does so in a song of beauty.

What happens then if the person who wishes to express love is a woman? The difficulty for her is of two kinds. The first is, how does she come to be able to write out her feelings at all? She has to have access to learning, sometimes specialised learning that takes many years to acquire. If people think that all poetry is based on classical examples, for instance, she has to go to a certain kind of school before she can dare make the special kind of noise that we call poetry.

Then there is also the question of how a woman can dare to expose herself in such an immodest way as by describing her sexual passion. Because the poet is always the aggressor. It doesn't matter what gender the poet is, the beloved is made passive by poetry, and the poet is always the person who initiates the encounter. The page is blank before the mark is made upon it.

It is all the more ironic, then, to consider that the greatest love poet of all time, according to some, was a woman. The first great love poet in Western culture is generally considered to be Sappho, who lived on the Greek island of Lesbos in the 7th century BC.

Her most famous poem, which is sometimes called the 'Ode to Anactoria', was discovered for the Western world when the text of Longinus 'On sublimity' was discovered in 1550. For 2000 years before that she was lost.

When this poem surfaced, the whole literate world of Europe was absolutely staggered.

ODE TO ANACTORIA

He is more than a hero

He is a god in my eyes –
the man who is allowed
to sit beside you – he

who listens intimately
to the sweet murmur of
your voice, the enticing

laughter that makes my own
heart beat fast. If I meet
you suddenly, I can't

speak – my tongue is broken;

a thin flame runs under
my skin; seeing nothing,

hearing only my own ears
drumming, I drip with sweat;
trembling shakes my body

and I turn paler than
dry grass. At such times
death isn't far from me

Sappho is known to most people because she lived on the isle of Lesbos, as a lesbian, a woman who made love to her own sex. She was also the mother of a daughter, whom she loved with great passion. That seems to indicate that at some stage in her life she was also a lover of men. There is no reason why one should actually exclude the other.

Sappho describes the physical sensations that the presence of the beloved brings about. Most of the poem is in terms of what is happening to her physically – her heart is pounding, she is sweating, she is afraid she might faint. They are all feelings that we know about. They are those feelings you used to have when you were crazy about somebody, who would turn your world upside-down just by coming into the room at a party.

You would think: Oh my goodness, everyone can see. If he or she came to you, and spoke to you, you would find to your horror that you were saying something really fatuous and foolish, that you were wasting your one opportunity.

It is wonderful that Sappho tells you with such understandability about that situation of complete impotence, looking at the person you love so wildly giving his (her) full attention to a lucky someone else. In describing her helplessness, however, Sappho takes the initiative. She makes the gesture. She extends her libido into a public space where other people can see it. That is a very risky proceeding – for a woman.

Ironically, boys studying the classics – that is, boys of

• DAVID (1748–1825), Sappho and Phaon

the ruling class in England and elsewhere in Europe – used to learn this poem, and they had to make their own translations. There were literally thousands of translations of this poem in existence, virtually all of them by men, in which men had to take upon themselves the impotence that Sappho felt looking at her beloved. Our translation, however, is by the distinguished woman poet and classical scholar, Mary Barnard

In the late 16th century, only noblewoman learned to read and write at all but, interestingly, they were often given the same education that young men had. Queen Elizabeth, for example, could read Latin and Greek. Lady Mary Wroth (c.1586–c.1652) had an even more special destiny because she was born into a family which would have been remarkable for its poetry in any era. Her uncle was Sir Philip Sidney, author of *Astrophel and Stella*, one of the most famous of the famous Elizabethan love-sonnet sequences. Her aunt was Mary Herbert, the Countess of Pembroke, to whom Sir Philip dedicated his huge novel *The Arcadia* and a poet in her own right. Lady Mary's father, Sir Robert Sidney, wrote a book of poems that his daughter knew almost by heart.

Lady Mary, it seems, fell in love with her cousin, William Herbert, who was one of dedicatees of Shakespeare's first folio, when she was still a little girl. Both of them had to make dynastic marriages, but it looks very much to me as if they remained in love with each other while they were married to other people. When Lady Mary was widowed, she did something most unusual for a noblewoman: she bore two children, love children, by the man she loved.

The situation was not easy for her, because Herbert was a bit of a womaniser and he seems, to me at least, to have been rather cold-hearted as well. The years of Lady Mary's widowhood seem to have been lonely and she spent some time unpacking her aching heart with words. In 1621 something extraordinary happened. Lady Mary had been writing a sequel to *The Arcadia* and that spring it appeared under the title of *The Countess of Montgomerie's Urania written by the right honourable the Lady Wroth*. As if this was not scandalous enough (for noblewomen, though they might write, should not publish) she included at the end a sonnet sequence from Pamphilia, 'the all-loving', to Amphilanthus, 'the man who loves everybody'. In it Lady Mary spelt out the story of her unhappy love.

In one of the poems, she describes a dream where she sees the triumph of Cupid. Cupid's triumph is, of course, over her. She sets out her situation as if it were a picture.

When night's blacke Mantle could most darknesse
proue,
And Sleepe (deaths Image) did my senses hyre,
From Knowledge of my selfe, then thoughts did
moue
Swifter then those, most swiftnesse neede
require?

In sleepe, a Chariot drawne by wing'd Desire,
I saw; where sate bright Venus *Queene of Loue,*
And at her feete her Sonne, still adding Fire
To burning hearts, which she did hold aboue,

But one heart flaming more then all the rest,
The Goddesse held, and put it to my breast,
Dear Sonne now thus, said she, thus must we
winne;

He her obeyd, and martyr'd my poore heart.
I waking hop'd as dreames it would depart,
Yet since, O me, a Louer I haue beene.

Lady Mary's idea that love is an accident, a disaster that befalls you, that you are in some kind of captivity, that it hurts and burns and that it's all the fault of a small blind god, a baby god, is developed further and with added pungency because she had children by the man she loved, without having access to the man

• RICCI (1676–1730), Venus and Cupid

himself. When she writes about weeping Cupid, she writes about him in a way that no man could possibly write about a baby god.

Loue a childe is euer crying,
Please him, and he strait is flying;
Giue him, he the more is crauing,
Neuer satisfi'd with hauing.

His desires haue no measure,
Endlesse folly, is his treasure:
What he promiseth, he breaketh,
Trust not one word that he speaketh.

Hee vowes nothing but false matter,
And to cousen you hee'l flatter:
Let him gain the hand, hee'l leaue you,
And still glory to deceiue you.

Hee will triumph in your wailing,
And yet cause be of your failing:
These his vertues are, and slighter
Are his guifts; his fauours lighter.

Feathers are as firme in staying,
Wolues no fiercer in their praying.
As a childe then leaue him crying,
Nor seeke him so giu'n to flying.

That poem is quite remarkable because love, the baby, and love, the baby's father, and love, the wingèd god, keep interchanging backwards and forwards. You know at the end when she says 'leave him crying' that she can no more leave him crying than a mother can ignore the crying of her infant.

Lady Mary Wroth was extraordinary by any standards. The next extraordinary woman to arise, who spoke about her own sexual passion with a new kind of frankness, was not a noblewoman. In fact, we really don't know where she came from. She has been called the first Englishwoman to make her living by her pen, but I'm not at all sure that Aphra Behn (1640–1689) was English, or that she ever really made a living by her pen. But she certainly wrote and she wrote wonderfully.

For Aphra Behn, sex was a social activity, a necessary accompaniment to the good life. She lived in the Restoration, at a time when English society was affected – I think much for the better – by the proximity and the influence of France, when men as well as women had a duty of attraction and had to look wonderful, with great flowing full-bottomed wigs, and high red heels to their shoes and wonderful glittering clothing, and very flourishing manners and very demonstrative emotional gestures and behaviours – which is what this poem is about.

In Imitation of Horace

What mean those Amorous Curles of Jet?
For what heart-ravisht Maid
Dost thou thy Hair in order set,
Thy Wanton Tresses Braid?
And thy vast Store of Beauties open lay,
That the deluded Fancy leads astray?

For pitty hide thy Starry eyes,
Whose Languishments destroy:
And look not on the Slave that dyes
With an Excess of Joy.
Defend thy Coral Lips, thy Amber Breath;

To taste these Sweets lets in a Certain Death.

Forbear, fond charming Youth, forbear,
Thy words of Melting Love:
Thy Eyes thy Language well may spare,
One Dart enough can move.
And she that hears thy voice and sees thy Eyes
With too much Pleasure, too much Softness, dies.

Cease, cease, with Sighs to warm my Soul,
Or press me with thy Hand:
Who can the kindling fire controul,
The tender force withstand?
Thy Sighs and Touches like wing'd Lightning fly,
And are the God of Love's Artillery.

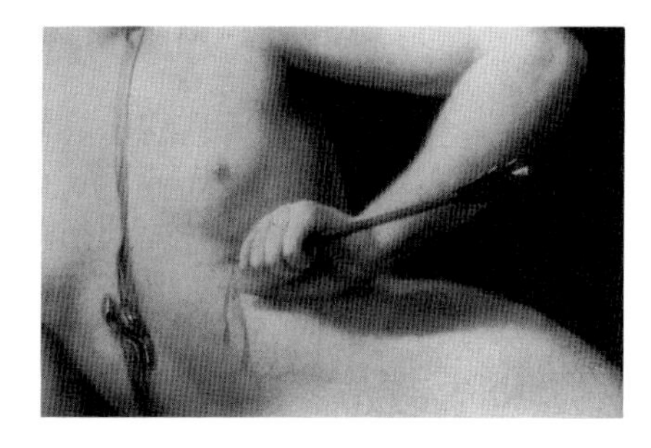

We are back in the land of Cupid and Cupid's arrows. The same kind of pictorial approach to passion that we saw in Lady Mary's poem is used again here, but in this case a very cunning and adroit social game is being played. The poet is saying, 'Oh, stop seducing me,' in terms that make it clear that what she means is, 'Go on, go on seducing me.' She is actually praising her own emotional potency at the same time that she celebrates the extraordinary attractiveness of her love object.

By the way, the word 'youth' that she uses there could be either male or female. Which it actually was really doesn't matter because what is important here is the manipulation of the relationship between the desirer and the desiree. Behn has herself, the poet desirer, taken on the attributes of the passive desiree in order to present her female passion in an acceptable guise. The obviousness of the strategy is part of the point.

Aphra Behn is also the author of a very famous song, which she included in one of her plays. This song is always included in collections of 17th-century lyrics because of its great style and swing. Again, its argument turns on a basic contradiction.

SONG

Love in Fantastique Triumph satt,
Whilst Bleeding Hearts around him flow'd,
For whom Fresh paines he did Create
And strange Tyranick power he show'd:
From thy Bright Eyes he took his fires,
Which round about in sport he hurl'd;
But 'twas from mine he took desires,
Enough t' undo the Amorous World.

From me he took his sighs and tears,
From thee his Pride and Crueltie;
From me his Languishments and Feares,
And every Killing Dart from thee.
Thus thou and I the God have arm'd
And sett him up a deity;
But my poor Heart alone is harm'd,
Whilst thine the Victor is, and free!

I find that poem wonderful, because Behn declares that the depth of her desire is enough to undo the amorous world – the whole world is amorous because love or desire is the basic motif that makes the world turn, according to Aristotelian and many other accepted ideas about creation. The poet takes upon herself the depth of desire which the flirtatious male object of desire – or female, it really doesn't matter – is free of, stating, without complaining about it, that in the battle of love the person who feels less must win.

Everybody knows the story of Elizabeth Barrett (1806–61), how she was a languishing, sickly woman who wrote wonderful poetry, locked up in a bedroom where she was in bed with her little dog, and how she was rescued by another poet, who had the extraordinary good taste and wonderfulness to love her for her poetry. This probably never happened on any other occasion before or since. The poet who loved her and married Elizabeth Barrett was Robert Browning.

In the course of their courtship, which was rather risky because Elizabeth's father seemed to be unwilling to allow his frail daughter to undergo the stresses and strains of matrimony, she wrote a series of sonnets about her love for Robert. The best-known of them is this one.

How do I love thee? Let me count the ways.
I love thee to the depth and breadth and height
My soul can reach, when feeling out of sight
For the ends of Being and Ideal Grace.
I love thee to the level of every day's
Most quiet need, by sun and candlelight.
I love thee freely, as men strive for Right;
I love thee purely, as they turn from Praise.
I love thee with the passion put to use
In my old griefs, and with my childhood's faith.
I love thee with a love I seemed to lose
With my lost saints—I love thee with the breath,
Smiles, tears, of all my life!—and, if God choose,
I shall but love thee better after death.

From *Sonnets from the Portuguese* (1850)

Well, you may say, what happened to sex? This is not exactly a turn-on, this kind of writing. Indeed, Robert might well have thought: Oh goodness, how am I going to function here? The beloved here is treated as some kind of saint or idol. He is the repository of all the love the poet has ever felt, of all her optimism, of all her desire, of all her ambition even. This man is going to have to be the justification of her life.

Something massive has happened between this kind of writing about love and Aphra Behn's. Aphra Behn sees sexual activity itself as an end worth pursuing, something worth promoting, but it looks as if Elizabeth Barrett, later Mrs Browning, is justifying her passion by likening it to something holy. How can you love someone 'better after death' – before the Last Judgement anyway – if you haven't got a body to do it with? Sex the one thing the poet doesn't mention in her list of ways she loves. But there is no mistaking the ('sincerity' is not the right word to use) concentration, the firmness of this statement of intent and belief. *I love you the right way, that is, I love you like this. I love you with no sense of humour whatsoever.*

What we have there, paradoxically, is the beginning of 20th-century sex religion, that makes your sexual partner into everything that you should require of any kind of companion: your best friend, your alter ego, your adviser, your saviour. This monomania carried within it the germs of its own disappointment. Elizabeth Barrett Browning was to write some bitter poetry about love and marriage before she died what was still a premature death at the age of 55.

Christina Rossetti (1830–94) was born 24 years after Elizabeth Barrett, but she inherited much of the same kind of intellectual and emotional baggage. She was encouraged to write poetry from the time she was a little girl. As a result of her family's indulgent praise, combined with a scanty formal education, she never formed any very clear idea of how much work is actually involved in creating a finished poem. It was said of Mrs Browning that she improved until the last day of her life. Christina, however, continued to work at more or less the same level. Her work reaches some pitches of intensity when dealing with subjects important to her, especially her family relationships, above all with her glamorous and exciting brother, Dante Gabriel Rossetti, and the woman in his life, Lizzie Siddal. Her most famous poem is *Goblin Market* (1862), which relates to her relationship with her siblings and her understanding of pleasure, desire, addiction and freedom.

When Rossetti was 27, she wrote an extraordinary poem, which relates in large measure to her own idea of her emotional potency, and the inadequacy of any human object to satisfy it.

THE HEART KNOWETH ITS OWN BITTERNESS

When all the over-work of life
Is finished once, and fast asleep
We swerve no more beneath the knife
But taste that silence cool and deep;
Forgetful of the highways rough,
Forgetful of the thorny scourge,
Forgetful of the tossing surge,
Then shall we find it is enough?

How can we say 'enough' on earth;
'Enough' with such a craving heart:
I have not found it since my birth
But still have bartered part for part.
I have not held and hugged the whole,
But paid the old to gain the new;
Much have I paid, yet much is due,
Till I am beggared sense and soul.

I used to labour, used to strive
For pleasure with a restless will:
Now if I save my soul alive
All else what matters, good or ill?

• ROSSETTI (1828–82), The Annunciation

I used to dream alone, to plan
Unspoken hopes and days to come—
Of all my past this is the sum:
I will not lean on child of man.

To give, to give, not to receive,
I long to pour myself, my soul,
Not to keep back or count or leave
But king with king to give the whole:
I long for one to stir my deep—
I have had enough of help and gift—
I long for one to search and sift
Myself, to take myself and keep.

You scratch my surface with your pin;
You stroke me smooth with hushing breath;—
Nay pierce, nay probe, nay dig within,
Probe my quick core and sound my depth.
You call me with a puny call,
You talk, you smile, you nothing do;
How should I spend my heart on you,
My heart that so outweighs you all?

Your vessels are by much too strait;
Were I to pour you could not hold,
Bear with me: I must bear to wait
A fountain sealed thro' heat and cold.
Bear with me days or months or years;
Deep must call deep until the end
When friend shall no more envy friend
Nor vex his friend at unawares.

Not in this world of hope deferred,
This world of perishable stuff;—
Eye hath not seen, nor ear hath heard,
Nor heart conceived that full 'enough':
Here moans the separating sea,
Here harvests fail, here breaks the heart;
There God shall join and no man part,
I full of Christ and Christ of me.

You have to wonder, in a poem like that, what the idea of Christ really contains. Christ is the most potent lover and the earthly lover is to be treated as Christ. Elizabeth Barrett treated her husband as a priest, and Christina Rossetti, failing a god for her spouse, chose solitude, but not silence. In her own life she published only the first and last stanzas of that poem. The hope of those women who long to recover their intellectual past is that, though she was not willing to reveal them in her lifetime, Rossetti did not throw the other revealing, arrogant, blasphemous stanzas away, that she kept them in trust for us to read and understand.

In the 20th century, women have been able to write about their own sexual feelings in lots and lots of

different ways, ironic, satiric, self-mocking, even obscene if they want to. But even when they seem to be at their most outrageous, the literary conventions are still there, embedded in every word they use, because every word in the language has been moulded by the way that it has been used in the past. Nowadays you could say that women are free to move around the poetic establishment at will. But it is a sobering reflection that, though we may number our poets in thousands these days, books of poetry, even best-selling ones, tend to sell in hundreds. It would be too bitter an irony to think that the tradition that was begun by Sappho would end in the 21st century with the collapse of print culture, before women had been able to explore its deepest, most poetic dimension.

FURTHER READING

A Book of Women's Verse edited by J.C.Squire (Oxford1921).

Kissing the Rod: An Anthology of Seventeenth-Century Women's Verse edited by G. Greer, S. Hastings, J. Medoff & M. Sansone (London 1988).

The World Split Open: Four Centuries of Women Poets edited by L. Bernikow (London 1979).

Sappho: A New Translation by Mary Barnard (Berkeley, Los Angeles, London 1958).

The Poems of Lady Mary Wroth edited by J. A. Roberts (London 1983).

The Works of Aphra Behn edited by Montague Summers (London 1915).

The Uncollected Verse of Aphra Behn edited by G. Greer (Stump Cross 1989).

'Aurora Leigh' and Other Poems introduced by Cora Kaplan (London 1978).

The Complete Works of Elizabeth Barrett Browning edited by Charlotte Porter - Helen A. Clarke (6 vols, New York 1900, AMS reprint 1973).

The Complete Poems of Christina Rossetti: A Variorum Edition edited with textual notes and introductions by R. W. Grump (London 1990).

A much more comprehensive bibliography on this topic is available on request. Send an SAE to:
Poetry Bibliography, Box 4000, London W3 6XJ.

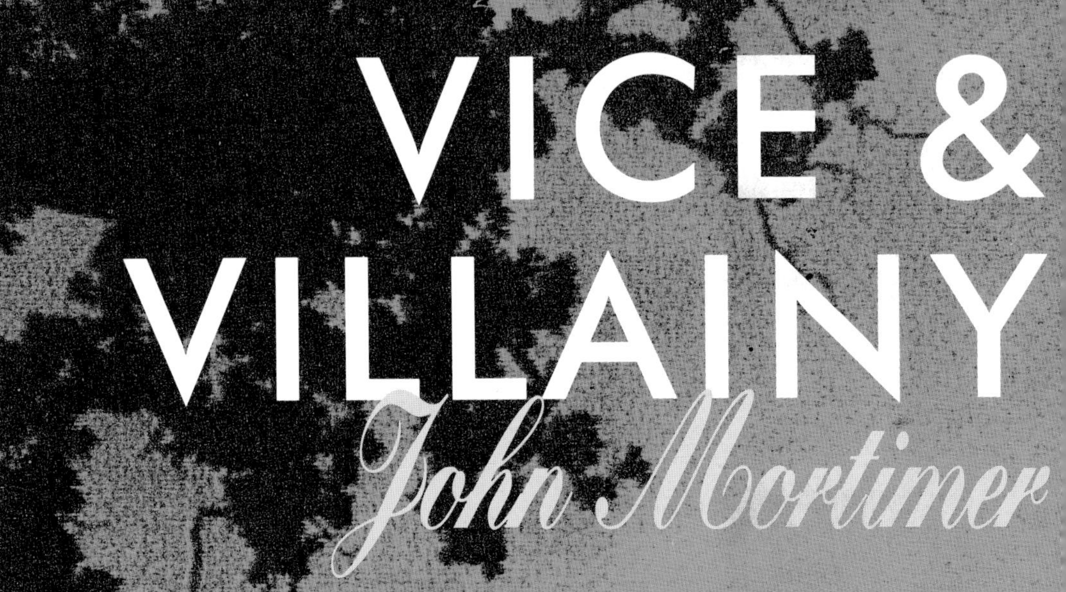
VICE &
VILLAINY
John Mortimer

As a barrister, John Mortimer is well known for his stand against censorship, and has achieved international fame as the author of the television series *Rumpole of the Bailey*. He first achieved literary prominence with his radio/television play *The Dock Brief* (1957) and the autobiographical stage and television play *Voyage Round My Father* (1970). He is also responsible for the television adaptation of Evelyn Waugh's *Brideshead Revisited* (1981) and John Fowles' *The Ebony Tower* (1985). Recent work includes the linked television mini-series *Paradise Postponed* and *Titmuss Regained*, as well as *Summer's Lease* (based on his novel).

Tlot-tlot, tlot-tlot! Had they heard it? The horse-hoofs ringing clear;
Tlot-tlot, tlot-tlot, in the distance! Were they deaf that they did not hear?

Down the ribbon of moonlight, over the brow of the hill,
The highwayman came riding,
Riding, riding!
The red-coats looked to their priming! She stood up, straight and still.

Tlot-tlot, in the frosty silence! Tlot-tlot, in the echoing night!
Nearer he came and nearer. Her face was like a light.
Her eyes grew wide for a moment; she drew one last deep breath,
Then her finger moved in the moonlight,
Her musket shattered the moonlight,
Shattered her breast in the moonlight and warned him – with her death.

He turned. He spurred to the west; he did not know who stood
Bowed, with her head o'er the musket, drenched with her own red blood!
Not till the dawn he heard it, and his face grew grey to hear
How Bess, the landlord's daughter,
The landlord's black-eyed daughter,
Had watched for her love in the moonlight, and died in the darkness there.

Back, he spurred like a madman, shouting a curse to the sky,
With the white road smoking behind him and his rapier brandished high.
Blood-red were his spurs i' the golden noon; wine-red was his velvet coat;
When they shot him down on the highway,
Down like a dog on the highway.
And he lay in his blood on the highway, with the bunch of lace at his throat.

And still of a winter's night, they say, when the wind is in the trees,
When the moon is a ghostly galleon tossed upon cloudy seas,
When the road is a ribbon of moonlight over the purple moor,
A highwayman comes riding—
Riding—riding—
A highwayman comes riding, up to the old inn-door.

From The Highwayman
by Alfred Noyes (1880–1958)

That is the romantic view of villainy. The highwayman asked innocent citizens for their money or their lives. He robbed and may have murdered, but to Alfred Noyes, he was a romantic hero.

This is a collection of poems about villains, the black hats, the bad guys. And it is a strange fact that people have always found them far more interesting than the white-hatted, thoroughly good fellows. That may be because villainy is far easier to write about – it is hard not to make goodness boring.

If we had had a hand in the Creation, we might well say that we should have not only made a world without earthquakes, or fatal diseases, but also one in which crime had never been invented. How delightful that would be, how safe, how calm, how free we should all be to eat muesli and discuss the Maastricht treaty. And then we should add, after only a few minutes' thought, `But, dear God, how dull!'

And would God have agreed? There was a time when I went around interviewing bishops and other clerics, including a cardinal, who were unable to provide what I regarded as a convincing explanation of the existence of evil. Only Malcolm Muggeridge came up with an idea that seemed to go anywhere near fitting the facts. He saw the Almighty as a master dramatist, a Shakespeare of the skies, who knows – as does any other pro – that a play without villains is likely to be extremely tedious. So this celestial playwright spends his time drawing up parts for Senator McCarthy, Dr Crippen and Mr Robert Maxwell.

But however fascinating these characters, don't we have to believe in some sort of spirit of evil? Can you have a God without a Devil? For Milton, in *Paradise Lost*, the Devil was still a romantic hero – an aristocrat, a Prince of Darkness. He couldn't be an underdog among the good. He chose a more heroic role, that of Sovereign in the Kingdom of Evil. This is Satan speaking . . .

Farewel happy Fields,
Where Joy for ever dwells: Hail horrours, hail
Infernal world, and thou profoundest Hell
Receive thy new Possessor: One who brings
A mind not to be chang'd by Place or Time.
The mind is its own place, and in it self

Can make a Heav'n of Hell, a Hell of Heav'n.
What matter where, if I be still the same,
And what I should be, all but less then Hee
Whom Thunder hath made greater? Here at least
We shall be free; th' Almighty hath not built
Here for his envy, will not drive us hence:
Here we may reign secure, and in my choyce
To reign is worth ambition though in Hell:
Better to reign in Hell, then serve in Heav'n.

From *Paradise Lost*, Book I (1658–63)

But does the Devil – the spirit of evil – always go around advertising himself, showing off his horns and his tail? Or can he, does he quite often, appear in a blue suit with an old school tie, looking, for all the world, like your friendly neighbourhood bank manager? W. H. Auden said, `Evil is unspectacular and always human/And shares our bed and eats at our own table.'

Percy Bysshe Shelley (1792–1822) was the most romantic of poets, a free spirit, an atheist, an anarchist – and an aristocrat. He had an impassioned belief in freedom, justice and truth and a great hatred for convention and conventional people, bad poets and politicians. Perhaps that is why, in this short section from *Peter Bell the Third* (1819), he saw the Devil as quite an ordinary chap.

The Devil, I safely can aver,
Has neither hoof, nor tail nor sting;
Nor is he, as some sages swear,
A spirit, neither here nor there,
In nothing – yet in everything.

He is – what we are; for sometimes
The Devil is a gentleman;
At others a bard bartering rhymes
For sack; a statesman spinning crimes;
A swindler, living as he can;

• BRUEGHEL (c. 1515–1569), The Triumph of Death (detail)

A thief, who cometh in the night,
With whole boots and net pantaloons,
Like some one whom it were not right
To mention; – or the luckless wight,
From whom he steals nine silver spoons.

But however wicked the Devil is, however much he flashes his wicked eyes and gives off a strong smell of sulphur and burning flesh, there are still human beings who can outdo him in villainy . . . and men and women who approach bad behaviour as one of the social graces. Such a person, undoubtedly, was Lady Poltagrue.

ON LADY POLTAGRUE, A PUBLIC PERIL
Hilaire Belloc (1870–1953)

The Devil, having nothing else to do,
Went off to tempt my Lady Poltagrue.
My Lady, tempted by a private whim,
To his extreme annoyance, tempted him.

If villainous characters are easier to write, if sinners fall more easily off the pen, they are certainly much more fun to act. Villains are the stars of stage and screen. Actors, in their simple and optimistic way, believe they should play parts in which the audience

loves them. They are wrong. The Devil has the best tunes and villains most of the best lines. Who would play Othello if Iago was on offer? Who would turn down Lady Macbeth in favour of Lady Macduff? Who would want to act that well-meaning but colourless character David Copperfield if you could have a stab at Uriah Heap? It is the villains who make the entertainment world go round. Can you imagine Red Riding Hood without the Wolf, or Snow White without the Wicked Queen? What a bore Robin Hood would be without the Sheriff of Nottingham. Richard III comes on to the stage and, after seducing a widow over her husband's coffin, proceeds to murder almost everyone in sight. There was hardly ever a better part written for an actor.

Shakespeare's villains sometimes try to excuse themselves. Richard III, who relishes his own villainy, says it is really a substitute for sex . . .

Why, I in this weak piping time of peace
Have no delight to pass away the time,
Unless to spy my shadow in the sun
And descant on mine own deformity.
And therefore since I cannot prove a lover
To entertain these fair well-spoken days,
I am determinèd to prove a villain . . .

Richard III, I, i, 24–30

Richard III's belief that his villainy was due to his not getting enough sex is a complaint that certainly could not be made by William Plomer's `French Lisette', the star of his `Ballad of Maida Vale'. Although women seem to commit fewer crimes than men – many male criminals take the old-fashioned view that a woman's place is in the home and not out robbing banks – villainy knows no sex barriers, and this poem shows what great con artists women can be. It also has the most ingenious rhyming scheme . . .

FRENCH LISETTE: A BALLAD OF MAIDA VALE
William Plomer (1903–73)

Who strolls so late, for mugs a bait,
In the mists of Maida Vale,
Sauntering past a stucco gate
Fallen, but hardly frail?

You can safely bet that it's French Lisette,
The Pearl of Portsdown Square,
On the game she has made her name
And rather more than her share.

In a coat of cony with her passport phony
She left her native haunts,
For an English surname exchanging her name
And then took up with a ponce.

Now a meaning look conceals the hook
Some innocent fish will swallow,
Chirping 'Hullo, darling' like a cheeky starling
She'll turn, and he will follow.

For her eyes are blue and her eyelids too
And her smile's by no means cryptic,
Her perm's as firm as if waved with glue,
She plies an orange lipstick,

And orange-red is her perky head
Under a hat like a tiny pie –
A pie on a tart, it might be said,
Is redundant, but oh, how spry!

From the distant tundra to snuggle under her
Chin a white fox was conveyed,
And with winks and leerings and Woolworth's
earrings
She's all set up for trade.

Now who comes here replete with beer?
A quinquagenarian clerk
Who in search of Life has left 'the wife'
And 'the kiddies' in Tufnell Park.

Dear sir, beware for sex is a snare
And all is not true that allures.
Good sir, come off it. She means to profit
By this little weakness of yours:

Too late for alarm! Exotic charm
Has caught in his gills like a gaff.
He goes to his fate with a hypnotised gait,
The slave of her silvery laugh,

And follows her in to her suite of sin,
Her self-contained bower of bliss,
They enter her flat, she takes his hat,
And he hastens to take a kiss.

Ah if only he knew that concealed from view
Behind a 'folk-weave' curtain
Is her fancy man, called Dublin Dan,
His manner would be less certain,

His bedroom eyes would express surprise,
His attitude less langour,
He would watch his money, not call her 'Honey'.
And be seized with fear or anger.

Of the old technique one need scarcely speak,
But oh, in the quest for Romance
'Tis folly abounding in a strange surrounding
To be divorced from one's pants.

One of the greatest, perhaps most underestimated poets is Robert Browning (1812–89). He was that rare thing – a poetic intellectual, full of ideas, but also a brilliant technician and sometimes extremely funny. He was also a great dramatist. Not in his plays – they are hard to read and probably impossible to act – but in a series of superb dramatic monologues. Browning was reluctant to write about himself and his own emotions, so he wrote beautifully in the characters of painters and prelates and – in this poem – a pathological murderer, one who kills for love and because of love. In an extraordinary way, Browning gets into the mind of such a killer, in a haunting poem with a last line of hair-raising simplicity.

PORPHYRIA'S LOVER

The rain set early in to-night,
The sullen wind was soon awake,
It tore the elm-tops down for spite,
And did its worst to vex the lake:
I listened with heart fit to break.
When glided in Porphyria; straight
She shut the cold out and the storm,
And kneeled and made the cheerless grate
Blaze up, and all the cottage warm;
Which done, she rose, and from her form
Withdrew the dripping cloak and shawl,
And laid her soiled gloves by, untied
Her hat and let the damp hair fall,
And, last, she sat down by my side
And called me. When no voice replied,
She put my arm about her waist,
And made her smooth white shoulder bare,
And all her yellow hair displaced,
And, stooping, made my cheek lie there,
And spread, o'er all, her yellow hair,
Murmuring how she loved me – she
Too weak, for all her heart's endeavour,
To set its struggling passion free
From pride, and vainer ties dissever,
And give herself to me for ever.
But passion sometimes would prevail,
Nor could to-night's gay feast restrain
A sudden thought of one so pale
For love of her, and all in vain:
So, she was come through wind and rain.
Be sure I looked up at her eyes
Happy and proud; at last I knew
Porphyria worshipped me; surprise
Made my heart swell, and still it grew
While I debated what to do.
That moment she was mine, mine, fair,
Perfectly pure and good: I found
A thing to do, and all her hair
In one long yellow string I wound
Three times her little throat around,
And strangled her. No pain felt she;
I am quite sure she felt no pain.
As a shut bud that holds a bee,
I warily oped her lids: again
Laughed the blue eyes without a stain.

And I untightened next the tress
About her neck; her cheek once more
Blushed bright beneath my burning kiss:
I propped her head up as before,
Only, this time my shoulder bore
Her head, which droops upon it still:
The smiling rosy little head,
So glad it has its utmost will,
That all it scorned at once is fled,
And I, its love, am gained instead!
Porphyria's love: she guessed not how
Her darling one wish would be heard.
And thus we sit together now,
And all night long we have not stirred,
And yet God has not said a word!

The murderers I had to deal with as a barrister were easy clients to get on with, usually polite and grateful for whatever you could do for them. I am not speaking of gang killers, or those who robbed with violence; most murders go on, like Christmas, in the family circle. They take place between husbands and wives or lovers, or between best friends. These criminals seemed to have reached a certain peace by murdering the one person in life they felt they had to kill. Sitting with them in cells, discussing the case, perhaps joking about the witnesses, it often seemed extraordinary that such apparently calm

and reasonable people could break through the great safety barrier of inhibition that prevents us from taking another person's life.

It was said of Dr Crippen that he was a kindly, modest and hospitable little man, endlessly tolerant of his impossible wife. He behaved with great dignity at his trial, only concerned for the acquittal of his mistress, and he faced death with quiet courage. And yet he brought himself to kill his wife, dismember her body and bury it under the cellar floor.

Herbert Rowse Armstrong was a gentle lawyer from the little town of Hay-on-Wye, who not only murdered his wife but attempted to do in a rival solicitor. His manners were so good that, when he passed his intended victim a poisoned scone at tea-time, he uttered the immortal words, `Excuse fingers.' Terrible moments of inhumanity are surrounded by the quiet and casual concerns of everyday life.

In 1895, Oscar Wilde (1856–1900) was sent to prison for indecent behaviour with consenting young men. The judge who sentenced him, who was well acquainted with rape, murder and armed robbery, said it was the worst case he had ever tried. Wilde's name was removed from the theatres where he – the most successful playwright in London, the author of the immortal *Importance of Being Earnest* – had his plays on. The darling of London society, the great wit and kindly raconteur, became `Convict C3' in Reading Gaol, and the prostitutes danced in the streets. A gentle butterfly had been shamefully broken on the wheel by a hypocritical and cruel society.

Wilde never recovered, but this experience did produce his best poem, *The Ballad of Reading Gaol* (1898), where he saw, with pity and horror, a lonely murderer, another man who had killed for love.

He did not wear his scarlet coat,
For blood and wine are red,
And blood and wine were on his hands
When they found him with the dead,
The poor dead woman whom he loved,
And murdered in her bed.

He walked amongst the Trial Men
In a suit of shabby grey;
A cricket cap was on his head,
And his step seemed light and gay;
But I never saw a man who looked
So wistfully at the day.

I never saw a man who looked
With such a wistful eye
Upon that little tent of blue

Which prisoners call the sky,
And at every drifting cloud that went
With sails of silver by.

I walked, with other souls in pain,
Within another ring,
And was wondering if the man had done
A great or little thing,
When a voice behind me whispered low,
'That fellow's got to swing.'

Dear Christ! the very prison walls
Suddenly seemed to reel,
And the sky above my head became
Like a casque of scorching steel;
And, though I was a soul in pain,
My pain I could not feel.

I only knew what hunted thought
Quickened his step, and why
He looked upon the garish day
With such a wistful eye;
The man had killed the thing he loved,
And so he had to die . . .

Everyone has their own private villain, the person who, out of the whole world, they hate most, despise most, see as the personification of falsity and evil. For John Dryden (1631–1700), it was the Duke of Buckingham, although he did not pay him the compliment of treating him as a devil, more as a malignant fool. George Villiers, the 2nd Duke of Buckingham, was a friend of Charles II whom, it was said, Buckingham initiated into the vices he himself had acquired. Buckingham dabbled in politics after the Restoration, but also aspired to be a general, a scientist (he thought he had discovered the philosopher's stone), a poet and a playwright. He died of a chill caught on the hunting field. Here his character is torn to pieces in John Dryden's satire *Absalom and Achitophel* (1681).

A man so various, that he seem'd to be
Not one, but all Mankind's Epitome.
Stiff in Opinions, always in the wrong;
Was Every thing by starts, and Nothing long:
But, in the course of one revolving Moon,
Was Chymist, Fidler, States-man and Buffoon;
Then all for Women, Painting, Rhiming,
Drinking,
Besides ten thousand Freaks that died in
thinking.
Blest Madman, who coud every hour employ,
With something New to wish, or to enjoy!
Railing and praising were his usual Theams;
And both (to shew his Judgement) in Extreams:
So over Violent, or over Civil,
That every Man, with him, was God or Devil.

In squandring Wealth was his peculiar Art:
Nothing went unrewarded, but Desert.
Beggar'd by fools, whom still he found too late:
He had his Jest, and they had his Estate.

Treason and treachery, spies and spymasters. These are difficult words to define. One man's traitor is another man's hero, just as `freedom fighters' are `terrorists' viewed from the other side of the battlefield. In the works of John Buchan and Ian Fleming, spies and

anti-spies are clubland heroes – and the English seem particularly addicted to this type of villainy. No doubt it has some snob appeal as so many of our traitors have been old public school boys and members of the Establishment. It is also a profession that, like acting and painting, seems to be its own reward. Perhaps the excitement is enough. People will betray their country and take enormous risks for the most trivial sums of money. They may be `perfect spies' but, as Gavin Ewart (1916–) suggests in this poem, quite inadequate people.

BRILLIANT SPY AND TOTALLY INADEQUATE MAN

Last seen in a bar called 'The Whore's Shoe'.
Gone fishing with an agent out of Prague.
A life constructed of episodes.
Notes on the piano, ambiguous to the last.

Nothing rhymes. It's just a syllable
count. It's Time that carries you on, from one
electric second of the clock's tick
to the next – and all it means is purely nothing.

Knitting is what it's like, long stories
where stitches link in line like woolly spies –
networks and cover, safe houses, who's
blown? Your mind must hold it all in place, like
knitting.

Boring it certainly is – and quite
fairly futile. Messages from Control
sometimes come through but praise is rare and
letter-placing arduous; from within, boring.

Mole. Into that foreign soil burrowed,
a fox among the Philistines – Nature
provides parallels, host/parasites;
so does History. Zeebrugge too had a mole.

Man you are and secret. If the cap
fits wear it. All you'll get from literates,
in human terms sad, this epitaph:
'brilliant spy and totally inadequate man.'

So what *is* this spirit of evil, this cause of villainy? Is it nature or nurture? Are villains born or made? No doubt poverty, hunger, the intolerable harshness of so many lives produce crime. But many criminals have come from comfortable and loving homes. It may be that the real cause of crime is the excitement of evil, the taking of the great risk, the tasting of the forbidden fruit. So, at the end, we are back to Satan, the great seducer, a softly spoken snake arising sinuously from the ground to tempt Eve, the first law breaker. Here is how Milton described the scene in *Paradise Lost*.

So spake the Enemie of Mankind, enclos'd
In Serpent, Inmate bad, and toward Eve
Address'd his way, not with indented wave,
Prone on the ground, as since, but on his reare,
Circular base of rising foulds, that tour'd
Fould above fould a surging Maze, his Head
Crested aloft, and Carbuncle his Eyes;
With burnisht Neck of verdant Gold, erect
Amidst his circling Spires, that on the grass
Floted redundant . . .

. . . With tract oblique
At first, as one who sought access, but feard
To interrupt, side-long he works his way.
As when a Ship by skilful Steersman wrought
Nigh Rivers mouth or Foreland, where the Wind
Veers oft, as oft so steers, and shifts her Saile;
So varied hee, and of his tortuous Traine
Curld many a wanton wreath in sight of Eve,
To lure her Eye: shee busied heard the sound
Of rusling Leaves, but minded not, as us'd
To such disport before her through the Field,
From every Beast, more duteous at her call,
Then at Circean *call the Herd disguis'd.*
Hee bolder now, uncall'd before her stood;
But as in gaze admiring: Oft he bowd
His turret Crest, and sleek enamel'd Neck,
Fawning, and lick'd the ground whereon she trod.

From *Paradise Lost*, Book IX

FURTHER READING

Readers wanting to pursue this theme further could do worse than to read Milton's *Paradise Lost*, Shakespeare's plays, the novels of Charles Dickens and Wilkie Collins, and Marjoribanks' *The Trials of Marshall Hall* (Penguin 1989). But perhaps the most convenient starting-point would be *The Oxford Book of Villains*, edited by John Mortimer (Oxford University Press, 1992).

• GOES (c. 1440–1482), The Fall (detail)

IN MEMORIAM
A.S. Byatt

Educated at York and at Newnham College, Cambridge, A. S. Byatt taught at the Central School of Art and Design and at University College London before becoming a full-time writer. Her literary criticism includes studies of Iris Murdoch and of Wordsworth and Coleridge, but since the publication of her first novel *Shadow of the Sun* in 1964, she has become far better known for her fiction: *The Game*, *The Virgin in the Garden*, *Still Life*, *Sugar and Other Stories* and *Angels and Insects*. In 1990, her novel *Possession* won both the Booker Prize and the *Irish Times*/Aer Lingus International Fiction Prize, and she was appointed a CBE.

MARKED WITH D Tony Harrison

When the chilled dough of his flesh went in an
oven
not unlike those he fuelled all his life,
I thought of his cataracts ablaze with Heaven
and radiant with the sight of his dead wife,
light streaming from his mouth to shape her
name,
'not Florence and not Flo but always Florrie'.
I thought how his cold tongue burst into flame
but only literally, which makes me sorry,
sorry for his sake there's no Heaven to reach.
I get it all from Earth my daily bread
but he hungered for release from mortal speech
that kept him down, the tongue that weighed like
lead.
The baker's man that no one will see rise
and England made to feel like some dull oaf
is smoke, enough to sting one person's eyes
and ash (not unlike flour) for one small loaf.

That was Tony Harrison's poem about his dead father. It is passionate and savage and witty. It is witty in the 17th-century sense – it plays with words and ideas to make a desperately serious point. The comparisons between the ovens where Harrison's father baked bread in his lifetime and the furnace in which his body was finally burned are brilliant verbal jokes, alive with the light and flame that are only punningly present in the dead man, blind and with a `cold tongue' becoming tongues of flame in death. In Harrison's poem – a formal sonnet into the bargain – verbal brilliance, intellectual play and genuine furious grief are perfectly fused.

Death brings out the poet in everyone. I think the idea of `rites of passage' – human formal celebrations of birth, puberty, marriage, death – is connected to the need to make poetry. We live in a culture that has taken away most of the formality of mourning – we are more likely to tell jokes or hold a party for the dead than to sing chants or weep ritually. And yet we need that formality.

When I judged the *TLS* poetry competition a few years ago, there were an enormous number of poems written by people who had sat by the deathbed of a child or a parent, who wanted to make a form for mourning. Most of these poems were very bad because

they lacked the verbal wit and beauty of Tony Harrison's poem. They ran away sluggishly into cliché, however painful the genuine feeling in them. A person who writes a good poem about death – or anything – has to care as much about language as about the subject matter. The vitality of the language balances the pain, even while it makes it more powerful.

The poems that follow are a mixture of formal public elegies – public grief – and personal poems about death. They are roughly in chronological order. The first, like Harrison's sonnet, is a personal cry of loss, given a very precise and witty form. *An Exequy to His Matchlesse Never to Be Forgotten Friend* was written by Bishop Henry King (1592–1669) for his young wife Anne who died in 1624.

Near the beginning, he writes, `I find out/How lazily time creeps about/To one that mourns,' and the beat of the poem itself mimics the inexorable progress of the ticking minutes or the pulse of the living – and dying – blood in the body. In one great metaphor, he compares his own pulse to the menacing drum of an advancing army. The following passage is the conclusion of the poem.

Sleep on my Love in thy cold bed
Never to be disquieted!
My last good night! Thou wilt not wake
Till I thy fate shall overtake:
Till age, or grief, or sickness must
Marry my body to that dust
It so much loves, and fill the room
My heart keeps empty in thy tomb.
Stay for me there: I will not faile
To meet thee in that hollow Vale.
And think not much of my delay:

I am already on the way,
And follow thee with all the speed
Desire can make, or sorrows breed.
Each minute is a short degree,
And ev'ry houre a step towards thee.
At night when I betake to rest,
Next morn I rise neerer my West
Of life, almost by eight houres saile,
Than when sleep breath'd his drowsie gale.
Thus from the Sun my Bottom stears,
And my dayes Compass downward bears.
Nor labour I to stemme the tide,
Through which to Thee I swiftly glide.
'Tis true; with shame and grief I yield:
Thou, like the Vann, first took'st the field,
And gotten hast the victory
In thus adventuring to dy
Before me, whose more years might crave
A Just precedence in the grave.
But heark! My pulse, like a soft Drum,
Beats my approch, tells Thee I come;
And slow howere my marches be,
I shall at last sit down by Thee.
The thought of this bids me go on,
And wait my dissolutïon
With hope and comfort. Dear (forgive
The crime) I am content to live
Divided, with but half a heart,
Till we shall meet and never part.

Another witty 17th-century poem, equally personal, equally formal, is the sonnet by the playwright Ben Jonson (1572–1637), written on the death of his first son at the age of seven. At that time, most families expected to lose one or more children, and one of the interesting emotions of Jonson's poem is the fear of caring too much, too painfully.

ON MY FIRST SON

Farewell, thou child of my right hand, and joy;
My sin was too much hope of thee, loved boy.
Seven years thou wert lent to me, and I thee pay,
Exacted by thy fate, on the just day.
Oh, could I lose all father, now! For why
Will man lament the state he should envy?
To have so soon scaped world's and flesh's rage,
And, if no other misery, yet age!
Rest in soft peace, and, asked, say here doth lie
Ben Jonson his best piece of poetry;
For whose sake, henceforth, all his vows be such,
As what he loves may never like too much.

Now one of the great formal elegies in English, or in any language – John Milton's *Lycidas* (1637). It was published with a collection of formal laments for Edward King, a student at Cambridge with Milton, who was

drowned on his way to Dublin – wrecked in calm weather.

The poem is written in an artificial pastoral form. The poet takes on the persona of a shepherd mourning another shepherd, Lycidas, and in the course of the poem, he meditates richly and strangely on life, death, ambition cut off, the Church, classical myths, his own hopes – in fact, everything except Edward King! And yet it is full of a kind of grief at the passing of things, and ends with one of the eternal themes of poetry: the sense that small human lives and deaths are part of some much larger whole that includes the earth, the tides, the water that killed the young man. *Lycidas* is a classical poem that ends with a Christian hope of heaven – a gracious reference to 'him that walked the waves', the Christ who walked on water and was resurrected. Again, the following comes from the conclusion of the poem.

Weep no more, woeful shepherds, weep no more,
For Lycidas, your sorrow, is not dead,
Sunk though he be beneath the wat'ry floor;
So sinks the day-star in the ocean bed,
And yet anon repairs his drooping head,
And tricks his beams, and with new-spangled ore
Flames in the forehead of the morning sky:

So Lycidas sunk low, but mounted high,
Through the dear might of him that walked the waves,
Where, other groves and other streams along,
With nectar pure his oozy locks he laves,
And hears the unexpressive nuptial song
In the blest kingdoms meek of joy and love.
There entertain him all the saints above,
In solemn troops and sweet societies
That sing, and singing in their glory move,
And wipe the tears for ever from his eyes.
Now, Lycidas, the shepherds weep no more;
Henceforth thou art the Genius of the shore,
In thy large recompense, and shalt be good
To all that wander in that perilous flood.

In *Lycidas*, the dead man becomes 'the Genius of the shore', part of nature. Perhaps the best poem I know about the sense that the individual human being comes out of the inanimate world and returns to it is a very short, simple one by William Wordsworth (1770–1850). It is so precise and bare that it is, at once, both personal and impersonal.

There are only two verses. In the first, the speaker is sealed into a kind of sleepy stillness by the sense of the untouchable life of the loved woman or girl. (We don't know anything about her except that she was once alive.) Love produces such false eternities. In the second verse, she is truly dead, the stillness is permanent, and there is a spare, hard, perfect line describing the way the dead return to the inanimate movement of the earth itself.

A slumber did my spirit seal;
It had no human fears:
She seemed a thing that could not feel
The touch of earthly years.

No motion has she now, no force;
She neither hears nor sees;
Rolled round in earth's diurnal course,
With rocks, and stones, and trees.

Lycidas is a long elegy. The epitaph is a brief form, with its own wit. Two of my favourites are the rueful one of Samuel Taylor Coleridge (1772–1834) for himself, and the magisterial one for Jonathan Swift written by William Butler Yeats (1865–1939).

Coleridge was obsessed with life in death and death in life – the two, in the form of horrible spectres, play dice for the Ancient Mariner's soul – and he saw his opium addiction as a long, drawn-out death in life.

Stop, Christian passer-by: Stop, child of God
And read, with gentle breast. Beneath this sod
A poet lies, or that which once seemed he –
O, lift a thought in prayer for S.T.C. –
That he who many a year with toil of breath
Found death in life, may here find life in death:
Mercy for praise – to be forgiven for fame –
He asked, and hoped through Christ. Do thou the
same.

And Yeats has used Swift's own phrase for the force behind his satire – *saeva indignatio*, `savage indignation' – in praise and pity.

Swift has sailed into his rest;
Savage indignation there
Cannot lacerate his breast.
Imitate him if you dare,
World-besotted traveller; he
Served human liberty.

The *In Memoriam* of Alfred, Lord Tennyson (1809–1892) is one of the greatest poems in the English language and, for the Victorians, a perfect summing up of their changing feelings about the world, religion, death, mourning and the life after death. It is a series of lyrics, written over a long period, prompted by the sudden death of Tennyson's great friend, Arthur Hallam, at the age of 23. It has many voices – savage, thoughtful, generalising, personal, beautiful, unpleasant.

I have chosen three of my favourite lyrics, all from the early part of the poem, partly because they fit in with the poems I have already included – the churchyard yew and the bald street and the dead hands tossed in water echo and deepen for us the water of *Lycidas* and the blank earthiness of the Wordsworth poem. Poems grow out of earlier poems, said T. S. Eliot, and change the way we see them.

Old Yew, which graspest at the stones
That name the under-lying dead,
Thy fibres net the dreamless head,
Thy roots are wrapt about the bones.

The seasons bring the flower again,
And bring the firstling to the flock;
And in the dust of thee, the clock
Beats out the little lives of men.

O not for thee the glow, the bloom,
Who changest not in any gale,
Nor branding summer suns avail
To touch thy thousand years of gloom:

And gazing on thee, sullen tree,
Sick for thy stubborn hardihood,
I seem to fail from out my blood
And grow incorporate into thee.

• • •

Dark house, by which once more I stand
Here in the long unlovely street,
Doors, where my heart was used to beat
So quickly, waiting for a hand,

A hand that can be clasp'd no more—
Behold me, for I cannot sleep,
And like a guilty thing I creep
At earliest morning to the door.

He is not here; but far away
The noise of life begins again,
And ghastly thro' the drizzling rain
On the bald street breaks the blank day.

• • •

I hear the noise about thy keel;
I hear the bell struck in the night:
I see the cabin-window bright;
I see the sailor at the wheel.

Thou bring'st the sailor to his wife,
And travell'd men from foreign lands;
And letters unto trembling hands;
And, thy dark freight, a vanish'd life.

So bring him: we have idle dreams:
This look of quiet flatters thus
Our home-bred fancies: O to us,
The fools of habit, sweeter seems

To rest beneath the clover sod,
That takes the sunshine and the rains,
Or where the kneeling hamlet drains
The chalice of the grapes of God;

Than if with thee the roaring wells
Should gulf him fathom-deep in brine;
And hands so often clasp'd in mine,
Should toss with tangle and with shells.

Another brief, perfect poem about the numbness after a death is by the American poet Emily Dickinson (1830–86), who was herself much obsessed by death – the coffin silks, the funeral plumes, the closed windows of houses, the unimaginable moment of the final loss of consciousness, the after-life of the body under the ground and the perhaps non-existent eternal life in heaven. `My Life Closed Twice' is wryly witty, like much of Dickinson's work. It is clear about the pain of death, and dubious about the promise of heaven.

My life closed twice before its close;
It yet remains to see
If Immortality unveil
A third event to me,

So huge, so hopeless to conceive
As these that twice befell.
Parting is all we know of heaven
And all we need of hell.

Finally, two modern elegies. W. H. Auden (1907–73) had many tones of voice: chatty, iconoclastic, lyric, funny. His two great elegies – for William Butler Yeats and (included here) for Sigmund Freud – are perfect examples of formal poetry with a plain, colloquial modern voice.

Freud died in September 1939, on the eve of the Second World War, and Auden's poem is an elegy for a whole threatened world and its wisdom. It is, as I have said, a modern poem, yet its brilliant last lines mourn Freud's rational intellect, and his understanding of irrational passions, in classical language in which it is not fanciful to hear the life of *Lycidas* persisting.

In Memory of Sigmund Freud

When there are so many we shall have to mourn,
when grief has been made so public, and exposed
to the critique of a whole epoch
the frailty of our conscience and anguish,

• Nazis and German students carrying 'un-Germanic' literature to the bonfires.

of whom shall we speak? For every day they die
among us, those who were doing us some good,
who knew it was never enough but
hoped to improve a little by living.

Such was this doctor: still at eighty he wished
to think of our life from whose unruliness
so many plausible young futures
with threats or flattery ask obedience,

but his wish was denied him: he closed his eyes
upon that last picture, common to us all,
of problems like relatives gathered
puzzled and jealous about our dying.

For about him till the very end were still
those he had studied, the fauna of the night,
and shades that still waited to enter
the bright circle of his recognition

turned elsewhere with their disappointment as he
was taken away from his life interest
to go back to the earth in London,
an important Jew who died in exile.

Only Hate was happy, hoping to augment
his practice now, and his dingy clientele
who think they can be cured by killing
and covering the gardens with ashes.

They are still alive, but in a world he changed
simply by looking back with no false regrets;
all he did was to remember
like the old and be honest like children.

He wasn't clever at all: he merely told
the unhappy Present to recite the Past
like a poetry lesson till sooner
or later it faltered at the line where

long ago the accusations had begun,
and suddenly knew by whom it had been judged,
how rich life had been and how silly,
and was life-forgiven and more humble,

able to approach the Future as a friend
without a wardrobe of excuses, without
a set mask of rectitude or an
embarrassing over-familiar gesture.

No wonder the ancient cultures of conceit
in his technique of unsettlement foresaw
the fall of princes, the collapse of
their lucrative patterns of frustration:

if he succeeded, why, the Generalised Life
would become impossible, the monolith
of State be broken and prevented
the co-operation of avengers.

Of course they called on God, but he went his way
down among the lost people like Dante, down
to the stinking fosse where the injured
lead the ugly life of the rejected,

and showed us what evil is, not, as we thought,
deeds that must be punished, but our lack of faith,
our dishonest mood of denial,
the concupiscence of the oppressor.

If some traces of the autocratic pose,
the paternal strictness he distrusted, still
clung to his utterance and features,
it was a protective coloration

for one who'd lived among enemies so long:
if often he was wrong and, at times, absurd,
to us he is no more a person
now but a whole climate of opinion

under whom we conduct our different lives:
Like weather he can only hinder or help,
the proud can still be proud but find it
a little harder, the tyrant tries to

make do with him but doesn't care for him much:
he quietly surrounds all our habits of growth
and extends, till the tired in even
the remotest miserable duchy

• WEYDEN (1399–1464), The Last Judgement, The Wicked in Hell (detail)

have felt the change in their bones and are cheered,
till the child, unlucky in his little State,
some hearth where freedom is excluded,
a hive whose honey is fear and worry,

feels calmer now and somehow assured of escape,
while, as they lie in the grass of our neglect,
so many long-forgotten objects
revealed by his undiscouraged shining

are returned to us and made precious again;
games we had thought we must drop as we grew up,
little noises we dared not laugh at,
faces we made when no one was looking.

But he wishes us more than this. To be free
is often to be lonely. He would unite
the unequal moieties fractured
by our own well-meaning sense of justice,

would restore to the larger the wit and will
the smaller possesses but can only use
for arid disputes, would give back to
the son the mother's richness of feeling:

but he would have us remember most of all
to be enthusiastic over the night,
not only for the sense of wonder
it alone has to offer, but also

because it needs our love. With large sad eyes
its delectable creatures look up and beg
us dumbly to ask them to follow:
they are exiles who long for the future

that lies in our power, they too would rejoice
if allowed to serve enlightenment like him,
even to bear our cry of 'Judas',
as he did and all must bear who serve it.

One rational voice is dumb. Over his grave
the household of Impulse mourns one dearly loved:
sad is Eros, builder of cities,
and weeping anarchic Aphrodite.

Auden perfectly combines the formal and the conversational voices. His is a civilised poem about a threatened civilisation. I want to end with a poem that completes a circle, in that it is poem of pure personal grief, contained in a regular form. It is `An Exequy' by Peter Porter (1929–), addressed to his own dead wife and deliberately written in the precise form invented by Bishop King, with which I began. Its tone is quite different, and yet it gains by being haunted by the ghost of the earlier poem, in its precise evocation of a particular modern grief. And I should also like to end where I began by meditating again on the paradox that

formal intelligence and the exciting use of language can both deepen grief and make it bearable, even beautiful.

I think of us in Italy:
Gin-and-chianti-fuelled, we
Move in a trance through Paradise,
Feeding at last our starving eyes,
Two people of the English blindness
Doing each masterpiece the kindness
Of discovering it – from Baldovinetti
To Venice's most obscure jetty.
A true unfortunate traveller, I
Depend upon your nurse's eye
To pick the altars where no Grinner
Puts us off our tourists' dinner
And in hotels to bandy words
With Genevan girls and talking birds,
To wear your feet out following me
To night's end and true amity,
And call my rational fear of flying
A paradigm of Holy Dying –
And, oh my love, I wish you were
Once more with me, at night somewhere
In narrow streets applauding wines,
The moon above the Apennines
As large as logic and the stars,
Most middle-aged of avatars,
As bright as when they shone for truth
Upon untried and avid youth

The rooms and days we wandered through
Shrink in my mind to one – there you
Lie quite absorbed by peace – the calm
Which life could not provide is balm

In death. Unseen by me, you look
Past bed and stairs and half-read book
Eternally upon your home,
The end of pain, the left alone.
I have no friend, or intercessor,
No psychopomp or true confessor
But only you who knew my heart
In every cramped and devious part –
Then take my hand and lead me out,
The sky is overcast by doubt,
The time has come, I listen for
Your words of comfort at the door,
O guide me through the shoals of fear –
'Fürchte dich nicht, ich bin bei dir.'

From 'An Exequy'

FURTHER READING

Bishop Henry King's poem can be found in *The Penguin Book of Metaphysical Verse*, edited by Helen Gardner. *The Penguin Book of Elizabethan Verse* is useful for Ben Jonson, and there is also a *Collected Poems* of Ben Jonson in Penguin. The great edition of Milton is the Longman annotated Milton, edited by Alistair Fowler and John Carey, but *Lycidas* can be found in many anthologies of English verse. There are many collections of Wordsworth – the Penguin is useful, and the Penguin parallel text of *The Prelude* in its early and late forms is a delight for the enthusiast. John Beer's Everyman edition of Coleridge is the most readable and helpful. Faber & Faber publish an excellent *Collected Poems of Emily Dickinson*, which is wonderful to read slowly, and a very good slim *Selected Poems*, edited by Ted Hughes.

The great edition of Tennyson is the Longman's annotated edition by Christopher Ricks, whose footnotes are a mine of interesting information, ideas and illuminating readings. There is a good Everyman edition, edited by John Jump, of *In Memoriam*, *Maud* and a few other poems. Macmillan have a paperback *Collected Poems* of Yeats, and Pan have a selected Yeats. Faber & Faber have published various collections of Auden – the *Collected Shorter Poems* includes the Freud elegy, and the equally moving Yeats elegy. There is also a very recent and excellent *Collected Poems*, edited by Edward Mendelson. Penguin publish a *Selected Poems* of Tony Harrison which is a good introduction to his work, and Oxford University Press publish many books of poems by Peter Porter, including a *Collected Poems,* which is perhaps the best place to start, and includes 'An Exequy'.

Large anthologies vary, according to the taste of the anthologist. My favourite was and is *The London Book of English Verse*, edited by Bonamy Dobree and Herbert Read – long out of print, I suspect. But if you see one in a second-hand bookshop, snap it up. The poems are brilliantly and enticingly arranged, and it is a good book to *read* as well as to dip into.

INDEX
OF POETS AND POEMS

GENERAL INFORMATION

For further information about poetry in general, the Poetry Library in London's Royal Festival Hall can offer a great deal of help. As well as the Saison Poetry Library of over 35,000 items and all the current poetry magazines, it can provide details (regularly updated) of poetry events and publications, competitions, groups and workshops, bookshops selling poetry, poet appreciation societies and so forth.

The Poetry Library
Royal Festival Hall, South Bank Centre
London SE1 8XX
Tel: (071) 921 0664/0943

If you live outside the London area, you could also try the following:

The Scottish Poetry Library
Tweedale Court, 14 High Street, Edinburgh EH1 1TE
Tel: (031) 557 2876

The Northern Arts Poetry Library
County Library, The Willows, Morpeth
Northumberland NE61 1TA

Poetry Ireland
The Austin Clarke Library
44 Upper Mount Street, Dublin 2, Eire

The literature officers of the various Regional Arts Boards in England and Wales can offer information on writers' groups and workshops, literary festivals, writers-in-residence and so on.
For a list of literature officers, send an A4 SAE to:
Research and Information Unit
The Arts Council
14 Great Peter Street, London SW1P 3NQ

For the same information in Scotland (where there are no regional boards), contact:
The Scottish Arts Council
12 Manor Place, Edinburgh EH3 7DD
Tel: (031) 226 6051

Finally, the Poetry Society in London organises poetry readings nationally, gives advice and information to practising poets, has an education department and publishes the quarterly Poetry Review. *Membership is open to anyone.*

The Poetry Society
22 Betterton Street, London WC2H 9BU
Tel: (071) 240 4810, Fax: (071) 240 4818